REAL WORLD DATA

GRAPHING NATURAL DISASTERS

Barbara A. Somervill

Chicago, Illinois

www.heinemannraintree.com
Visit our website to find out more information about Heinemann-Raintree books.

To order:

☎ Phone 888-454-2279

🖥 Visit www.heinemannraintree.com to browse our catalog and order online.

Edited by Megan Cotugno and Diyan Leake
Designed by Victoria Bevan and Geoff Ward
Original illustrations © Capstone Global Library, LLC 2010
Illustrated by Geoff Ward
Picture research by Mica Brancic, Q2AMedia
Originated by Chroma Graphics (Overseas) Pte Ltd
Printed in China by Leo Paper Products Ltd

14 13 12 11 10
10 9 8 7 6 5 4 3 2 1

Library of Congress Cataloging-in-Publication Data

Somervill, Barbara A.
  Graphing natural disasters / Barbara A. Somervill.
    p. cm. -- (Real world data.)
  Includes bibliographical references and index.
  ISBN 978-1-4329-2622-9 (hc) -- ISBN 978-1-4329-2631-1
(pb) 1. Natural disasters--Juvenile literature.. 2. Graphic
methods--Juvenile literature.. I. Title.
  GB5019.S66 2009
  363.34072'8--dc22
                          2009001290

Acknowledgments

The author and publishers are grateful to the following for permission to reproduce copyright material: Alamy p. **18** (Mountain Light/Galen Rowell); Corbis pp. **4** (Lu Zhanhong), **8** (Ryan Pyle); Dreamstime p. **6** (Juliengron); Getty images p. **16** (China Photos/Stringer); iStockphoto pp. **22** (cinoby), **25** (© Warwick Lister-Kaye); NOAA Photo Library pp. **12**, **14**, **26**; Office of Public Affairs p. **15** (niu.edu); Photolibrary p. **24** (Adrian Bailey); Reuters pp. **10** (Luis Enrique Ascui), **20** (STR New).

Cover photograph of floods in New Orleans, Louisiana, USA in the aftermath of Hurricane Katrina, reproduced with permission of Corbis (© US Air Force, digital version © Science Faction).

We would like to thank Dr. Ramesh Srivastava for his invaluable help in the preparation of this book.

Every effort has been made to contact copyright holders of any material reproduced in this book. Any omissions will be rectified in subsequent printings if notice is given to the publisher.

All the Internet addresses (URLs) given in this book were valid at the time of going to press. However, due to the dynamic nature of the Internet, some addresses may have changed, or sites may have changed or ceased to exist since publication. While the author and Publishers regret any inconvenience this may cause readers, no responsibility for any such changes can be accepted by either the author or the Publishers.

CONTENTS

Some words are printed in bold, **like this**. You can find out what they mean by looking in the glossary, on page 30.

WHAT ARE NATURAL DISASTERS?

Natural disasters happen on land, in water, and in the air. Some natural disasters happen because of the way the Earth is formed. These **geological** disasters include **volcanoes**, **earthquakes**, and **tsunamis**. Bad weather also causes natural disasters. Too much wind and rain come with **hurricanes**, **cyclones**, and **tornadoes**. Too much rain and melting snow cause floods. A lack of rain is just as bad. It causes **drought**. Humans can also cause natural disasters. This is true in the cases of most **avalanches** and some wildfires.

What are graphs?

This book uses graphs to show information about natural disasters. Graphs show information, or data, visually. There are many different types of graphs, but all graphs make it easier to see patterns at a glance. One small graph can give the same information as many pages of data.

 Floods destroy homes, personal property, and crops.

After a natural disaster, people need help. Help can be food, water, shelter, or medicine. It can be rebuilding homes, opening schools, or burying the dead. As well as loss of life or injury, natural disasters cause damage to property and loss of property. Every year, natural disasters cost billions of dollars.

The current **trends** in natural disasters tell a sad story. The number of incidents is increasing. Most scientists believe that **global warming** is causing the increase. Because the storms are more frequent and more powerful, the amount of damage and property loss from natural disasters is also increasing. The good news is that loss of life is decreasing. Early warning systems are saving lives.

U.S. natural disasters, 2006

The table below shows the loss of property from natural disasters in the U.S. in 2006. The bar graph shows the same information. The graph makes it instantly clear that flooding causes the most property damage.

Event	Property Damage in $ Million	Event	Property Damage in $ Million
Lightning	63.8	Fire	192.4
Tornado	752.3	Blizzard	571.0
Flash Flood	2,136.6	Drought	138.0
River Flood	1,631.1		

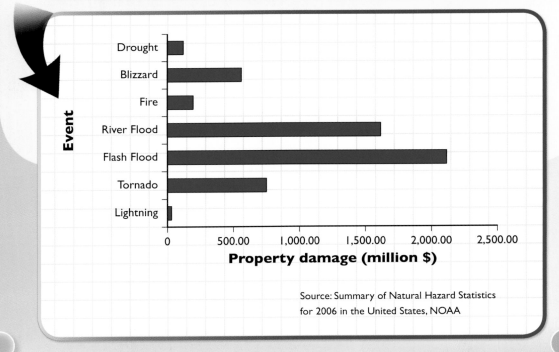

Source: Summary of Natural Hazard Statistics for 2006 in the United States, NOAA

VOLCANOES

Volcanoes send sparks, clouds of ash and dust, smoke, and lava shooting into the sky. They are dramatic and dangerous. An **eruption** can quickly destroy everything in the surrounding area.

Volcanoes can take many shapes. Some are gentle domes, called shield volcanoes. Some are cone-shaped mountains. When an eruption occurs, **magma** escapes through a hole in the volcano. The magma may shoot out with great force or ooze from the opening. Magma that flows over the Earth's surface is called lava. Some volcanoes may throw up clouds of super-heated ash, dust, and rock. These are called **pyroclastic** clouds. A pyroclastic explosion is as destructive and deadly as flowing lava.

 The lava seen in this photo may be as hot as 1,200 °C (2,200 °F).

Volcanic eruptions destroy forests and crops. They fill the air with ash, **pollute** water, and kill livestock. Buildings and forests are burned by lava or covered in ash and **debris**.

When Mt. Vesuvius blew its top in 79 CE, ash buried the Roman cities of Pompeii and Herculaneum. The 1883 eruption of Krakatoa blew up two-thirds of the island it sat on. The Soufrière Hills volcano on the Caribbean island of Montserrat has been erupting since 1995, making a large part of the island **uninhabitable**.

The most destructive volcano ever?

In 1815, Mt. Tambora, Indonesia, erupted. Ninety-two thousand people died because of the eruption. It disrupted weather around the world. Throughout the Northern hemisphere, snow fell in June, frost formed in July, and crops failed. Another 100,000 people died of hunger because Mt. Tambora's eruption caused a "year without a summer."

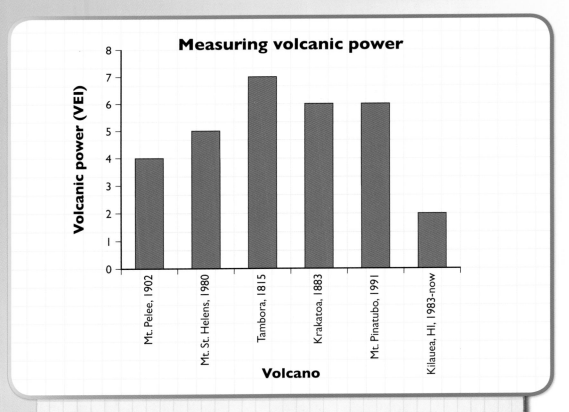

Measuring volcanic power

Volcanic power (VEI) vs. Volcano

- Mt. Pelee, 1902: 4
- Mt. St. Helens, 1980: 5
- Tambora, 1815: 7
- Krakatoa, 1883: 6
- Mt. Pinatubo, 1991: 6
- Kilauea, HI, 1983-now: 2

 Volcanic power is measured by the Volcanic Explosivity Index (VEI). The index ranges from non-explosive (0) to the most powerful (8). The bar graph shows that Tambora, Krakatoa, and Pinatubo eruptions were powerful eruptions.

Earthquakes shake, stretch, roll, and crack the Earth's crust. The Earth is not one solid block of land. It is many blocks, called **tectonic** plates. These plates move, although the movement happens over millions of years.

As plates push or pull on the Earth, they cause cracks, called **fault** lines. Pressure from the plates may cause the Earth to slip, slide, or shift along fault lines. As blocks of earth slip and slide, earthquakes occur. There are more than a million earthquakes every year. Humans do not feel most of them.

Measuring the power of an earthquake

The shaking of an earthquake is measured on a machine called a **seismograph**. The movement is shown as a zigzag line, called a seismogram. The stronger the quake, the closer and longer the zigzags appear on a seismogram. Scientists pinpoint the location where the earthquake starts. That point is called the **epicenter**. Scientists use the Richter scale to explain the **magnitude**, or power, of an earthquake. Those earthquakes that rate a 2 on the Richter scale usually can't be felt. A 7 is a serious, destructive earthquake.

 Earthquakes can crack roads and destroy bridges.

No one knows when an earthquake will strike. The earth shakes. Water and electricity lines break. Buildings crumble. Often people become trapped under rubble from falling buildings. In May 2008, Sichuan, China, experienced a 7.9 magnitude earthquake. Nearly 90,000 people were killed. More than 5 million buildings collapsed. Millions of people were left homeless.

The Richter scale: magnitude of earthquakes	Average number of events yearly
8 and higher	1
7–7.9	17
6–6.9	134
5–5.9	1,319
4–4.9	13,000 (estimated)
3–3.9	130,000 (estimated)
2–2.9	1,300,000 (estimated)

Seismograph

This diagram shows the seismic wave generated by an earthquake in Alabama. The nearly straight line indicates a normal seismic pattern—nothing is happening. As the line becomes more jagged, the earthquake is beginning. The section that shows sharp peaks and valleys shows earthquake activity.

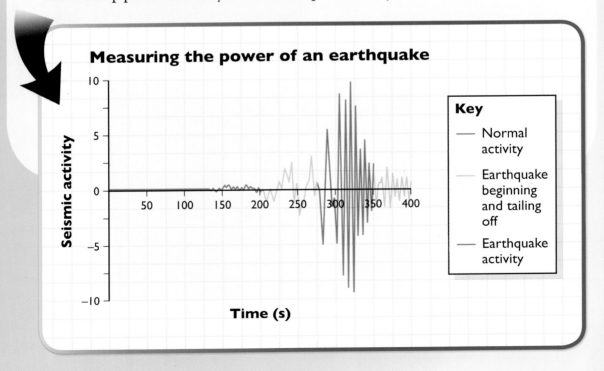

Measuring the power of an earthquake

Key
— Normal activity
— Earthquake beginning and tailing off
— Earthquake activity

Earthquakes and volcanic eruptions may cause tsunamis. Tsunamis are giant waves. They begin on the ocean floor and roll to shore. Waves can travel as fast as 720 kilometers (450 miles) per hour in the open ocean. They can measure as high as 30 meters (100 feet) tall. Or, they can be barely 1 meter (3 feet) high.

Like earthquakes, tsunamis have an epicenter. This is the point where a tsunami starts. A tsunami may be just one wave, but it is most often a series of waves. The waves travel in all directions from the epicenter toward the shore.

Disastrous damage

When a tsunami strikes, powerful waves crush buildings and trees along the shore. People caught by the wave may die or be seriously injured. Bridges are washed away. The salt water affects the fresh water supply and destroys crops. People who survive the waves are usually in desperate need of fresh water, food, and shelter.

 The tsunami that hit Asia in 2004 caused massive damage. Below is a photo of Phuket, Thailand, in the aftermath of the wave.

On December 26, 2004, the worst tsunami in recent years struck. An earthquake off the coast of Indonesia sent a shockwave through the Indian Ocean. A massive tsunami crashed into the shores of nearby Thailand, India, Sri Lanka, and Indonesia. Those shores are flat and heavily populated. People in the area had little warning before the tsunami hit.

Hundreds of thousands of people died or were injured. Whole towns disappeared under a sea of water and mud. The people living there lost everything. Affected areas needed water, food, clothing, medical help, temporary housing, and transportation.

The 2004 tsunami

This map shows the movement of the tsunami that struck Thailand in 2004. The line along the bottom is a line graph. It shows the change in the height of water level during a tsunami. The crest of the wave was the highest peak. The line graph shows several tall peaks. The wave drew so much water that the water level in front of it, the trough, was far below sea level.

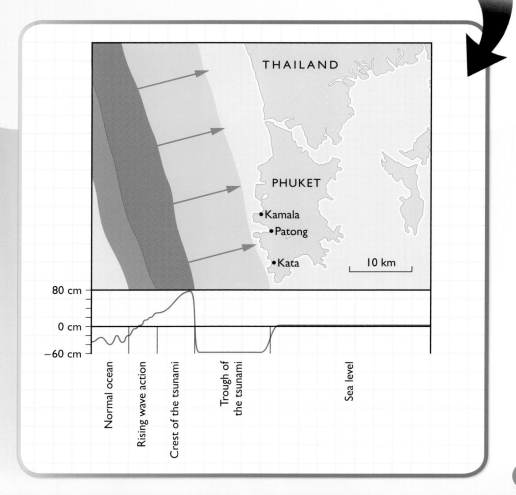

HURRICANES AND CYCLONES

A cyclone is a large mass of rotating air. The rotation is counter-clockwise in the Northern hemisphere and clockwise in the Southern hemisphere. When the surface winds exceed a certain value, they are called hurricanes or typhoons—hurricanes if they originated over the Atlantic or Pacific oceans and typhoons if they originated in Asia.

Hurricanes

Hurricanes are born in warm tropical waters. The storm gathers heat and energy over warm water. It builds in strength and destructive power as it moves along its path.

Hurricane Katrina

Hurricane Katrina struck New Orleans, Louisiana, in 2005. Katrina was not the most powerful hurricane ever to strike land, but it did become a very serious natural disaster. New Orleans is a city built on low-lying land and is protected by **levees**. Katrina's storm surge pushed water over and through the levees and flooded the city. Officials had asked people to leave the city, but many did not go. After the hurricane, rescue efforts were disorganized. There was no way to help the people in need who had remained in the city.

 Hurricane Katrina's storm surge flooded many Louisiana streets.

A hurricane spins around its center point, called the eye. The area protecting the eye is the eye wall. That is where the strongest winds blow. The wind churns around, carrying heavy rain. As a hurricane moves, it pushes ocean water ahead of it. This water, called a **storm surge**, floods the land before the hurricane strikes.

Hurricanes are classified in categories. The wind speed in a hurricane determines in which category the hurricane falls. The weakest hurricane (category 1) has wind speeds from 119 to 153 kilometers (74 to 95 miles) per hour. The most powerful hurricane is a category 5, with wind speeds over 249 kilometers (155 miles) per hour. Today, hurricanes are more frequent and more powerful than they have ever been before. Most scientists believe that the number of storms is increasing because of global warming.

There are three basic reasons why hurricanes and cyclones cause fewer deaths than they did 100 years ago. First, weather **forecasters** warn people of coming storms days in advance. When officials have a good idea where the storm will strike, they order people to leave the danger zone. After the storm, rescue efforts are usually well organized.

The Saffir-Simpson Scale

A hurricane's power is measured on the Saffir-Simpson scale. This graph is a pictogram of that scale. It uses pictures to represent the wind speed for each category of hurricane. The dark blue picures show the minimum wind speed for each category. The light blue pictures show the maximum.

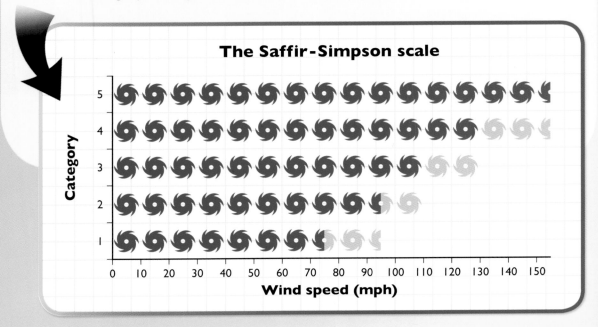

The Saffir-Simpson scale

TORNADOES

A tornado is a violent rotating windstorm. Thunder, lightning, rain, and hail may come with tornadoes, but the real problem is the wind. Tornadoes happen when warm, wet air smashes into cool, dry air. The crash of the two types of air creates huge thunderstorms. This is the ideal situation for a tornado to form.

The United States National Weather Service issues tornado watches and warnings, but no one can say for certain when or where a tornado will strike. No one can say how long it will last or how much damage it will do. A tornado can destroy a house on one side of the street and leave the house opposite untouched. Tornadoes are very unpredictable.

Measuring tornadoes

Tornadoes are measured by their wind speed and the extent of the damage they cause. These determine where a tornado lies on the Fujita–Pearson scale, which is used for measuring the strength of a tornado.

Tornadoes are easy to recognize. They form the shape of a funnel.

Tornadoes occur on every continent except Antarctica. From Australia to South Africa, Bangladesh to Brazil, the right conditions can produce the whirling air that creates a tornado.

Heavy tornado activity occurs every year in central North America. This area, called Tornado Alley, covers most states between the Rocky Mountains in the west and the Appalachian Mountains in the east. Tornado Alley averages 1,214 tornadoes in the U.S. and fewer than 100 in Canada every year.

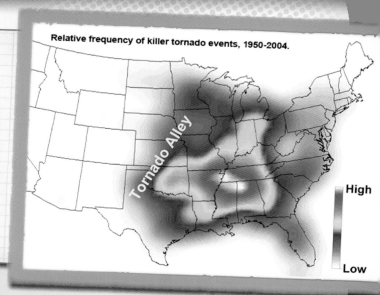

Relative frequency of killer tornado events, 1950-2004.

Tornado Alley

High

Low

Fujita–Pearson Scale	F–0	F–1	F–2	F–3	F–4	F–5
Lowest wind speed (mph) (kph)	40 64	73 117	113 182	158 254	206 331	261 420
Highest wind speed (mph) (kph)	72 116	112 180	157 253	205 330	260 418	318 512

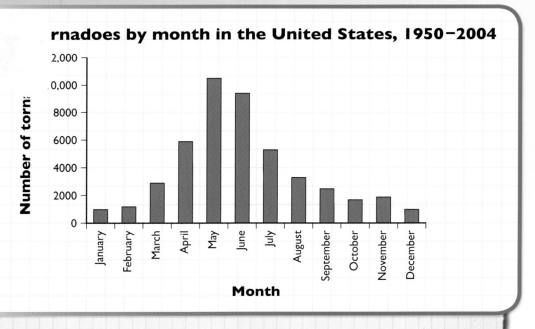

rnadoes by month in the United States, 1950–2004

Number of torn:

Month

The bar graph above shows the total number of tornadoes, by month, in the United States from 1950 to 2004. The months when there are the most tornadoes are May and June.

FLOODS

Throughout history, floods have been destructive and deadly natural disasters. Great floods left their mark on the land long before humans walked the earth. Flooding was a natural part of life.

A flood is basically water that overflows its container. The container could be riverbanks, lakeshores, dams, levees, or dikes. Heavy rainfall may cause flooding, such as in Sudan in 2007 and China in 2008. Broken dams, dikes, or levees also cause floods. A broken dam in Nepal in August 2008 forced thousands of people to flee their villages. Floods can also be caused by tsunamis and storm surges from hurricanes. They sweep over the land and flatten everything in their way.

 This flood in China in 2008 filled city streets with water.

Officials usually try to control flooding. Dikes hold the North Sea back and stop it from flooding millions of acres of farmland in the Netherlands. Levees and dikes contain the flow of the Mississippi River and other rivers. Dams on rivers restrict water flow and form lakes. These impressive constructions reduce the risk of flooding, but do not stop it completely.

In 2008, several events led to flooding in Chengdu, China. Heavy rains over-filled local lakes and rivers. China suffered the worst flooding in 50 years. Seventeen million people living in the region were affected. The floods destroyed crops and forced more than a million people to leave their homes.

Water-related disasters worldwide, 1990–2001

These pie charts show two types of information. The first pie chart shows water-related disasters throughout the world. You can see that floods make up 50% of all water-related disasters. The second pie chart shows where water-related disasters take place. Most take place in Asia (35%), followed by Africa (29%), and the Americas (20%).

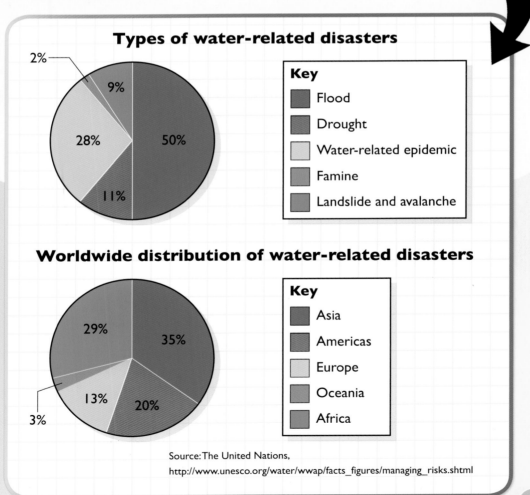

Types of water-related disasters

2%
9%
28%
50%
11%

Key
- Flood
- Drought
- Water-related epidemic
- Famine
- Landslide and avalanche

Worldwide distribution of water-related disasters

29%
35%
13%
20%
3%

Key
- Asia
- Americas
- Europe
- Oceania
- Africa

Source: The United Nations,
http://www.unesco.org/water/wwap/facts_figures/managing_risks.shtml

AVALANCHES

An avalanche is a snow slide down a mountainside. Avalanches happen mostly in late winter or early spring. Most avalanches occur on mountain slopes that lie at 30° to 45° angles.

Several factors cause avalanches. They happen shortly after a heavy snowfall that dumps 30 centimeters (1 foot) of snow or more. The extra snow puts stress on snow already on the ground. Several days of warm weather may melt the snow underneath and weaken the snow pack.

Even with all the above factors in place, an avalanche may not take place. Something extra, a trigger, usually starts an avalanche. Triggers range from the amount of snow and sunshine there is, to falling rocks, earthquakes, and noisy skiers. Ninety percent of victims of avalanches were the triggers that started the slide. Once an avalanche begins, the snow rushes downhill at speeds of around 150 kilometers (93 miles) per hour.

 An avalanche carries snow, ice, trees, rocks, and even people down a mountainside.

In the Alps, Rockies, and other mountain ranges, rangers identify possible avalanche sites. They then trigger small avalanches to control the amount of danger and loss of life from these natural disasters.

The avalanche danger scale

People who visit snowy mountain areas need to be aware of the danger codes that warn of possible avalanches. In most countries, black warns of extreme danger, followed by red (high), orange (considerable), yellow (moderate), and green (low). Canada uses red with a black border for extreme avalanche danger.

Avalanche triggers

As the pie chart below shows, 90 percent of avalanches are triggered by the victims of the avalanches themselves. Snowmobilers, snowboarders, and skiers trigger the majority of avalanches.

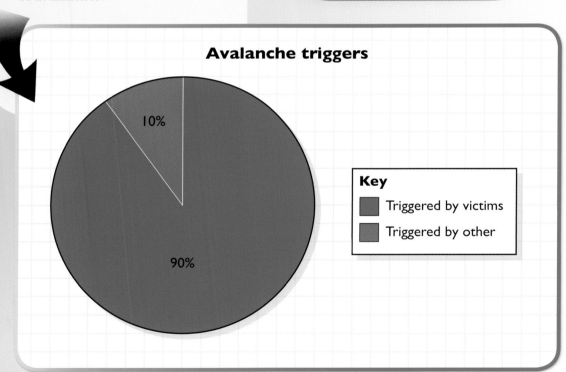

Avalanche triggers

10%

90%

Key

▪ Triggered by victims
▪ Triggered by other

LANDSLIDES

Landslides happen all over the world, including underwater. Landslides can be small trickles of pebbles and soil. They can also be massive flows of mud, rock, and plants. They can damage property, cause deaths, and cut off transportation links.

Many different factors can cause landslides. Heavy rain turns soil to mud, and the mud can slip downhill. Earthquakes and volcanic eruptions send rocks and earth tumbling. Building on unstable ground or the act of building roads and homes disrupts the soil. Whenever soil or rock on a hillside is disturbed, the possibility of a landslide exists.

Landslides are measured in cubic kilometers of material moved. After a landslide, getting rid of the material that has moved in the landslide is expensive. In 1998, the San Francisco Bay Area of California suffered heavy rains. The rains caused seven damaging landslides. The cost of clearing the dirt and debris was $140 million.

 A mudslide in Guatemala in 2005 left more than 600 people dead and hundreds more missing.

Human cost

The true measure of damage caused by a landslide is the lives lost and property damaged. In 1998, Hurricane Mitch caused landslides in Honduras, Guatemala, Nicaragua, and El Salvador. More than 10,000 people were killed as heavy rains sent rivers of mud flowing over towns and villages. People had no food, water, or shelter. The landslides cut off roads and damaged airports. Rescuers had difficulty reaching people who needed help.

The number of deaths from landslides in 2007

This bar graph compares the number of deaths from landslides in different countries in 2007. The graph shows that China had many more deaths from landslides than other nations, followed by Indonesia and India.

Country	Number of Deaths	Country	Number of Deaths
Afghanistan	43	Mexico	74
Bangladesh	150	Nepal	168
Brazil	56	Pakistan	273
China	677	Peru	40
Colombia	72	Philippines	92
India	352	Vietnam	130
Indonesia	465		

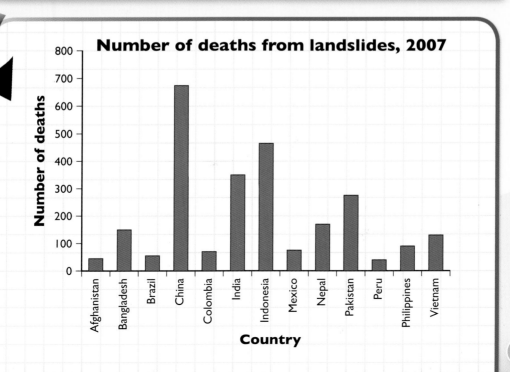

DROUGHT

Too much water is dangerous, but too little water is just as bad. Water is necessary for all life. A long-term lack of water is called a drought. Widespread drought means crops don't grow. For millions of people, the loss of even a single crop means **starvation**.

Drought happens when there is low **precipitation** over a long time period. Drought can happen on any continent and in any conditions. In 2005, the worst drought in 40 years affected the Amazon rainforest, a place where rain normally falls almost every day. Australia has suffered drought for many years. Water use is carefully restricted across the country. And, the entire continent of Africa is struggling to overcome many years of drought.

 People cannot grow food or crops in the dried, cracked soil of drought-hit areas of Africa.

No crops, no food!

The first effect of a drought is crop failure. When crops fail, people go hungry. If the drought lasts too long, topsoil may be blown away by the wind. When rain does come, it carries more topsoil from the land. **Erosion** creates new problems. By the time the drought ends, the quality of the soil is too poor to grow crops.

In 2000, Kenya suffered the worst drought in 60 years. The loss of crops affected 4 million people. In some areas, precious inches of topsoil were lost. Attempts to grow crops after the drought had ended failed. The problems Kenya faces are only a small part of how drought affects Africa. The World Food Bank and food aid agencies try to help. They deliver food and water to the most seriously affected areas. Although people try to help them, more than 16 million Africans are on the edge of starvation.

Major drought events, 1849–present

The timeline below shows some of the major periods of drought in different areas of the world.

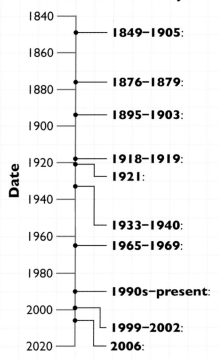

Timeline of major drought events, 1849–present

Date	Event
1849–1905:	Long-term drought strikes Arizona, lasting more than 50 years.
1876–1879:	Three-year drought leaves 9 million Chinese dead from starvation.
1895–1903:	Drought reduces Australian cattle numbers by 40%.
1918–1919:	Drought in Iran causes massive crop failure.
1921:	The Volga River basin drought brings on famine in Russia that kills more people than all the deaths in World War I.
1933–1940:	Drought reduces the Great Plains to a Dust Bowl.
1965–1969:	Prolonged drought in northern Africa contributes to the expansion of the Sahara Desert.
1990s–present:	Recurring drought leads to famine in Djibouti, Eritrea, Ethiopia, Kenya, Somalia, and Sudan.
1999–2002:	Drought in the southwest U.S. leads to an increase in wildfires.
2006:	Australia is gripped by the worst drought in 100 years.

Wildfire is a part of nature's plan. Natural wildfire most often begins from lightning strikes. Some natural wildfire starts from volcanic eruptions. Every year, natural wildfires burn forests, grasslands, and croplands.

People also start wildfires. Some of these fires are accidents, while others are acts of **arson** or are planned fires to clear land. Globally, humans burn up to 8.2 square kilometers (3.2 million square miles) of forest and grassland every year.

Good or bad?

Wildfire is both good and bad. On the good side, wildfire renews nature. The fire clears undergrowth and dead plant matter. The ash makes the soil more fertile. After a fire, new growth sprouts. Plant eaters feast on the new grass, and the **environment** comes back to life. Grasslands and other wilderness areas depend on fire to keep their environments healthy.

In 2009, the drought-stricken state of Victoria, Australia, suffered intense wildfires. More than 170 people died and billions of dollars were lost. The fires continued burning weeks after they started.

 This white stork has landed in wildfire in the Serengeti Plains of Africa.

Burning Yellowstone

In 1988, more than 486,000 hectares (1.2 million acres) of Yellowstone National Park burned in a wildfire. The fire was so intense that it burned a 250-year-old lodgepole pine in 15 seconds. Twenty years later, animal and plant species are thriving. Yellowstone's recovery after such a massive wildfire changed global views on managing wildfires. In many regions, natural wildfires burn without human interference.

Grasslands recover quickly from wildfire

This photograph shows the recovery of the Serengeti Plains after it has been struck by wildfire. Within months after the fire, new plants have sprouted. Within three years, the recovery will be well on its way, with full plant cover and a variety of animals.

One way that humans get ready for a natural disaster is by being warned that it may happen before it actually does. **Technology** today tells weather forecasters when storms are coming. The weather forecasters then warn people through television and radio. In some places, sirens blast warnings to say that disaster is on the way. It doesn't matter how people find out about natural disasters, just finding out is the important thing. Warnings save lives.

 Weather forecasters use Doppler radar to track storms so they can warn people about dangerous weather patterns.

Using technology

Local weather stations use Doppler **radar** units to decide about weather. A radar unit sends out radio waves from an antenna. The radio waves strike objects in the air, such as raindrops or snowflakes. When the waves hit the objects, they bounce back to the antenna. Rain may be hours away from the antenna. The farther away the rain is, the longer it takes for the radio waves to return to the antenna. As the rain approaches, the signals return sooner. Weather forecasters use the patterns of radio waves to decide how large a storm is and how fast it is moving.

Satellites orbiting the Earth provide pictures covering larger areas. The satellites carry instruments to scan the Earth. The instruments collect data that can be used to produce images of clouds. Cloud movement appears on the scans. This is how weather satellites track the paths of storms, hurricanes, and cyclones.

Seismographs record the Earth's movement in volcanic eruptions, earthquakes, and tsunamis. The records do not tell when an event will happen. They only record the energy spent as the event happens.

Scientists continue to develop new and better instruments to help predict possible natural disasters. As the ability to track natural disasters gets better, more lives can be saved.

Natural disasters, 1980-2003

Insurance companies recorded 13,700 natural disasters worldwide between 1980 and 2003. The pie chart shows the **proportion** of each group of disasters to the whole number.

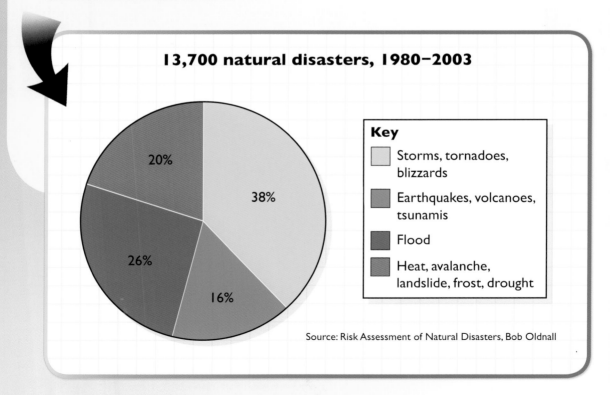

13,700 natural disasters, 1980–2003

20%

38%

26%

16%

Key

Storms, tornadoes, blizzards

Earthquakes, volcanoes, tsunamis

Flood

Heat, avalanche, landslide, frost, drought

Source: Risk Assessment of Natural Disasters, Bob Oldnall

CHART SMARTS

Data are bits of information about something. We get data as a list of facts or a mass of numbers. It can be difficult to understand large amounts of data. Graphs and charts are ways of displaying information visually. We can see relationships and patterns in data presented in graphs and charts. The type of chart used depends on the data that needs to be represented.

Pie charts

A pie chart is used to show the different parts of a whole picture. A pie chart is the best way to show how something is divided up. These charts show information as different-sized portions of a circle. They can help you compare proportions. You can easily see which section is the largest "slice" of the pie.

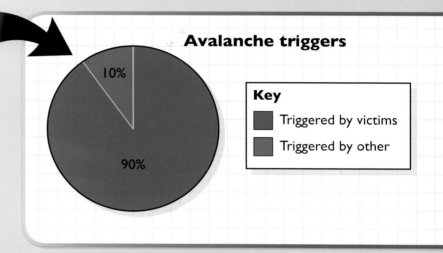

Avalanche triggers

10%

90%

Key
- Triggered by victims
- Triggered by other

Line graphs

Line graphs use lines to connect points on a graph. They can be used to show how something changes over time.

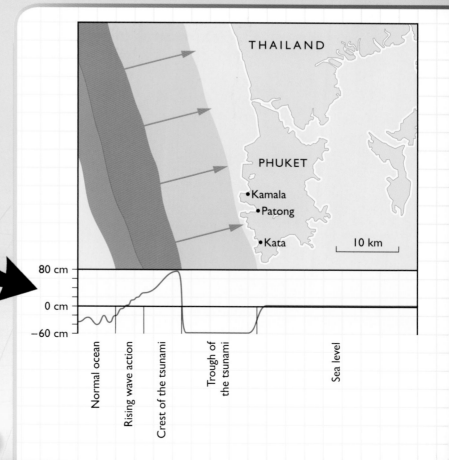

THAILAND

PHUKET

• Kamala
• Patong

• Kata

10 km

80 cm

0 cm

−60 cm

Normal ocean

Rising wave action

Crest of the tsunami

Trough of the tsunami

Sea level

Pictograms

A pictogram uses pictures or icons to represent information in a graph. Each icon represents a number of items. A pictogram might represent people, animals, or plants. In a graph about natural disasters, icons might represent clouds or wind speed.

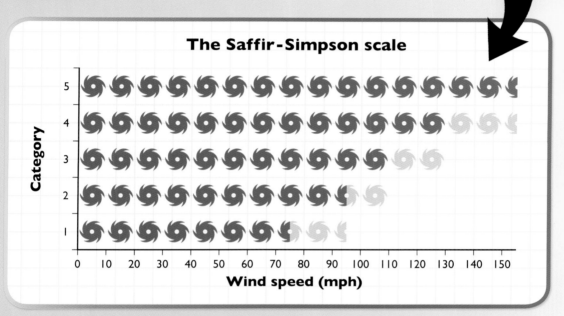

The Saffir-Simpson scale

Category / Wind speed (mph)

Bar graphs

A bar graph is a good way to compare amounts of different things. Bar graphs have a horizontal **x-axis** and a vertical **y-axis**. The x-axis usually shows the items being compared. The y-axis shows the scale of comparison.

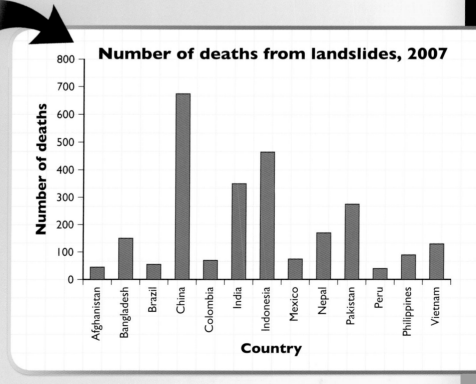

Number of deaths from landslides, 2007

Number of deaths / Country

GLOSSARY

arson criminal act of deliberately setting a fire

avalanche mass of snow and ice falling quickly down a mountainside

cyclone violent storm with heavy rain and violent wind

debris dirt or loose natural material, such as broken pieces of rock

drought period of time with little or no rain, snow, hail, or sleet

earthquake sudden violent shaking of the ground

environment surroundings or conditions in which a person, animal, or plant lives

epicenter focal point where an earthquake or tsunami begins

erosion process of soil or rock loss caused by wind, water, or other agents

eruption sudden explosion of a volcano

fault extended break in a body or rock

forecaster person who predicts or estimates the weather

geological to do with the Earth and its formation

global warming gradual increase of the overall temperature of the Earth's atmosphere

hurricane storm with heavy rain and violent wind

landslide sliding of earth or rock from a mountain or cliff

levee embankment built to stop a river overflowing

magma super-heated rock from beneath the Earth's surface

magnitude how large or serious something is

pollute add harmful substances to air, water, or soil

precipitation rain, hail, snow, or sleet that falls to the ground

proportion size of a group of data compared to other groups, or to the whole set of data

pyroclastic heated gas, ash, and rock from a volcano

radar electrical instrument for finding the presence, direction, distance, or speed of objects

satellite human-made object placed in orbit around the Earth

seismograph instrument that measures and records details of earthquakes

starvation suffering or dying from hunger

storm surge ocean water that is pushed on to land by a hurricane

technology use of scientific knowledge for practical purposes

tectonic relating to the basic structure of the Earth's crust

tornado mobile, destructive, rotating wind storm

trend general direction in which ideas or actions develop or change

tsunami large wave started by a volcano, landslide, or earthquake on the ocean floor

uninhabitable not fit for people to live in

volcano mountain or hill through which hot gas, lava, and rock fragments are thrown into the air

x-axis horizontal line on a graph

y-axis vertical line on a graph

FURTHER INFORMATION

Books

Ceban, Bonnie J. *Floods and Mudslides: Disaster & Survival.* Berkeley Heights, NJ: Enslow Publishing, 2005.

Fradin, Dennis, and Judith Fradin. *Witness to Disaster: Hurricanes.* Washington, D.C.: National Geographic Children's Books, 2007.

Grace, Catherine O'Neill. *Forces of Nature: The Awesome Power of Volcanoes, Earthquakes, and Tornadoes.* Washington, D.C.: National Geographic Children's Books, 2004.

Morris, Ann, and Heidi Larson. *Tsunami: Helping Each Other.* Minneapolis, Minn.: Lerner Publications, 2005.

Oxlade, Chris. *Violent Skies: Hurricanes.* Chicago: Raintree, 2005.

Woods, Michael, and Mary B. Woods. *Droughts (Disasters Up Close).* Minneapolis, Minn.: Lerner Publications, 2006.

Websites

Track the paths of current hurricanes and get more information about hurricanes and cyclones.
http://www.nhc.noaa.gov/

What do you do in the event of a natural disaster? How can you be disaster-ready? This website tells you everything you need to know.
http://www.fema.gov/kids/

Check out the National Geographic Society's information on natural disasters. Read the latest stories and see videos and photos of wildfires, avalanches, hurricanes, and more.
http://environment.nationalgeographic.com/environment/natural-disasters/

Where do natural disasters strike? See maps and read information collected by NASA's Earth Observatory about natural hazards.
http://earthobservatory.nasa.gov/NaturalHazards/

INDEX